THE PERFECTIONISM JOURNAL

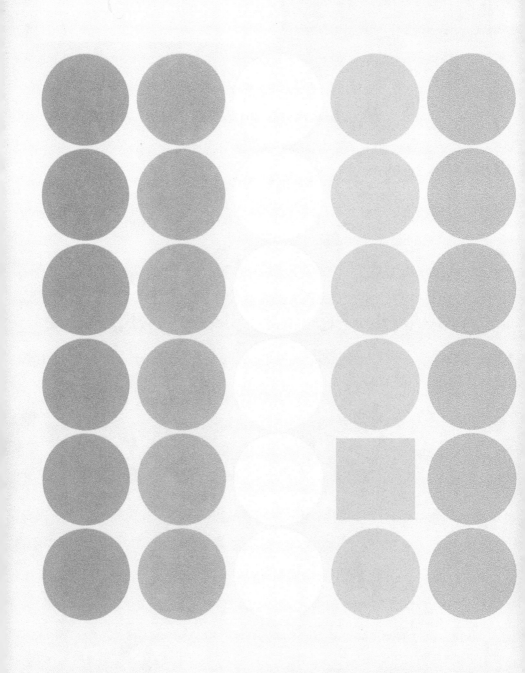

THE PERFECTIONISM JOURNAL

Guided Prompts and Mindfulness Practices
to Reduce Anxiety and Find Calm

TINA KOCOL, LPC

ROCKRIDGE
PRESS

Interior and Cover Designer: Stephane Mautone
Art Producer: Megan Baggott
Editor: Chloe Moffett
Production Manager: Jose Olivera
Production Editor: Melissa Edeburn

Paperback ISBN: 978-1-63878-586-6

R0

THIS JOURNAL BELONGS TO:

CONTENTS

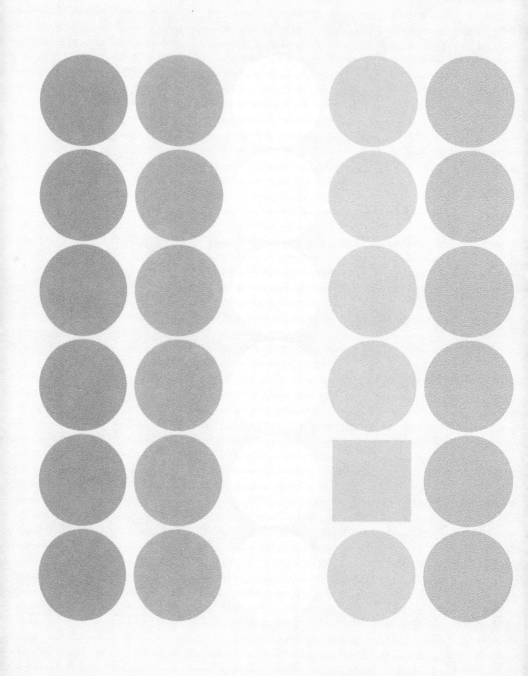

INTRODUCTION

Because you've decided to pick up this journal, I think it's safe to say that perfectionism plays a part in your life. It might be true that in several areas of your life, having perfectionist tendencies is beneficial. Maybe you've had success with personal or career goals you've set for yourself. Others may admire or notice your drive and dedication when it comes to tackling a project.

Perfectionism definitely has an upside, but every pancake has two sides.

You're likely interested in this journal because you've found yourself in a place where you can't achieve your way out. You don't take time to enjoy your accomplishments because you're already thinking about the next goal. You've tried improving yourself and/or others, but all that's doing is leaving you feeling anxious, exhausted, lonely, and frustrated.

If that sounds like you, you're in the right place.

Welcome! I'm Tina. I'm a licensed professional counselor, and I've been helping people work through issues of perfectionism for many years. Perfectionism is sneaky and shows up in unexpected ways when it goes unidentified and unchecked. I've seen clients whose perfectionism has manifested as anxiety, depression, low self-esteem, addiction or other compulsive behavior, self-harm, chronic stress, codependency, and/or disordered eating. At the core of my perfectionist clients, they lack trust in themselves and others. They're not satisfied or genuinely connected in their lives—even if they've become conventionally "successful."

Perfectionism is when you have specific expectations that you or the people around you must live by and there's only one "right" way to do something. Oftentimes, perfectionists are seen as achievers, so their standards go unchecked. But beliefs about how things should and shouldn't be can become so rigid and inflexible that relationships, work, and self-esteem are shattered when things aren't perfect. Perfectionism impacts many parts of life and actually prevents you from achieving your goals in the long run.

Perfectionism develops as a coping mechanism because of an emotional wound or a damaged relationship. Perfectionists create their own rules or adopt them from others to keep themselves safe and protected from their own or others' feelings of disappointment, guilt, anger, or shame. The problem with perfectionism is that it works . . . until it doesn't. When perfectionism stops working to ward off unwanted emotions, perfectionists feel even more stress and get stuck because perfectionism was the thing that kept those feelings at bay.

HOW TO USE THIS BOOK

This book is a resource to explore your perfectionistic tendencies, increase your appreciation for yourself, and learn to trust your instincts. Like any great adventure, exploring your inner self—your thoughts, feelings, and actions—can have some ups and downs. That's completely normal and, frankly, expected.

This journal is designed for you to explore how perfectionism impacts your life. Each theme includes writing prompts, exercises, and practices. The writing prompts will help you think differently about yourself and your perfectionism. The exercises are designed to dive deeper into the theme. The practices will help you to use the information you gained from the writing prompts and exercises in your everyday life.

As a perfectionist, you're probably focused on the end result, but this journal is about the *process*, not the *product*. Taking the time to investigate yourself through this journal is a different kind of outcome. Diving deeper into your perfectionism can help you be a more authentic version of yourself—you don't have to be trapped in the role of perfectionist anymore. Even after you complete the journal, you may find it beneficial to come back to certain questions, practices, or activities later because you'll have a new perspective on the themes based on your new experiences. You are a work in progress, and I hope you come to embrace the many parts of yourself that emerge in this journal.

Perfectionism measures our beginner's work against the finished work of masters.

—JULIA CAMERON

UNDERSTANDING
YOUR
PERFECTIONISM

Perfectionism isn't something that develops overnight. It usually begins as a way to protect yourself from unpleasant outcomes in life and gets reinforced in various ways. Can you remember when your perfectionism started? What events were happening? Who were you close to? What was going well for you? What was going wrong for you?

_____

_____

_____

_____

_____

_____

_____

_____

_____

_____

_____

_____

_____

_____

_____

_____

_____

_____

_____

As a perfectionist, you likely have high expectations for yourself. What are some expectations you hold yourself to? These could be in any area of your life—work, school, relationships, etc. Are your expectations realistic? Why or why not? Do you hold others to the same standards? Why or why not?

Perfectionism can be reinforced in your life by people who love you and mean well. They may make comments about how easy you make things look, your attractiveness or beauty standards, or how important success and achievement are to a happy life. How has perfectionism been reinforced in your life by other people? What are some things you've learned over the years from other people that have led you to believe that being perfect is an asset in life?

_____

_____

_____

_____

_____

_____

_____

_____

_____

_____

_____

_____

_____

_____

_____

_____

_____

Feeling the pressure to be perfect can create "black and white" thinking—that is, seeing the world as binary: good or bad, perfect or imperfect. Binary thinking can cause us to believe that there are only certain ways to do things. Is there anything in your life that you're very particular about? Has having those standards helped? Have they caused stress?

_____

_____

_____

_____

_____

_____

_____

_____

_____

_____

_____

_____

_____

_____

_____

_____

_____

_____

Perfectionism often leads to a sense of control and usually means a person is able to set and achieve goals. In what ways has being a perfectionist benefited you?

_____

_____

_____

_____

_____

_____

_____

_____

_____

_____

_____

_____

_____

_____

_____

_____

_____

_____

You've likely found that something about how you're living life as a perfectionist isn't working for you anymore. What is an incident or situation that's led you to question the role of perfectionism in your life?

EXPERIENCING
YOUR FEELINGS

1. Sit in a quiet, comfortable place and begin by taking a few deep breaths.

2. Review your answer to the prompt on page 2 about how perfectionism first showed up in your life.

3. Allow yourself to experience the emotions that came up for you as you read the memories.

4. Bring your attention to the emotion that feels the strongest or most prominent.

   - What are other times in your life that you've experienced that emotion prominently?

   - Is it a pleasant or unpleasant emotion for you?

   - What body sensations are you experiencing?

   - Where in your body do you feel the sensations?

5. Complete this practice with some deep, calming breaths, and thank yourself for being willing to sit with and experience these strong emotions.

WHAT TYPE OF PERFECTIONISM DO I HAVE?

There are three types of perfectionism. This assessment will help you learn which types of perfectionism you gravitate toward. Answer questions with "Yes" or "No."

Y | N

☐ ☐ 1. I work on projects until they are the best quality.

☐ ☐ 2. I feel bad when I make a mistake.

☐ ☐ 3. It bothers me when I know I could do better.

☐ ☐ 4. I feel better about myself when I am successful.

☐ ☐ 5. I have negative opinions about people that "settle" in careers, relationships, or their health.

☐ ☐ 6. It bothers me when people don't try their best.

☐ ☐ 7. When I delegate something, it is important that it is done to my standards.

☐ ☐ 8. I would never date or marry someone who didn't want to better themselves.

☐ ☐ 9. I have a reputation for excellence and people expect me to deliver.

☐ ☐ 10. I don't like to admit when I've made a mistake.

☐ ☐ 11. I worry others won't like me if I am not trying hard.

☐ ☐ 12. I want to be seen as successful to my friends and family.

If you answered mostly "Yes" to questions one through four, you tend toward **self-oriented perfectionism**.

Self-oriented perfectionism is when you have high standards for yourself, and you feel disappointed in yourself if you don't get things "right."

If you answered mostly "Yes" to questions five through eight, you tend toward **other-oriented perfectionism**.

Other-oriented perfectionism is when you have high standards for others, which can become unreasonably high. You feel let down and question the strength of relationships when others don't meet your expectations.

If you answered mostly "Yes" to questions nine through twelve, you tend toward **social-oriented perfectionism**.

Social-oriented perfectionism is when you feel pressure from others to be perfect. The pressure can come from family, friends, teachers, coaches, or other influential people in your life. Sometimes the pressure comes from the expectation that you should be a perfect representative of your culture or social circle.

It's common for perfectionists to display more than one kind of perfectionism, and sometimes perfectionism is circumstantial. Gaining awareness of the type of perfectionism you tend toward can help you identify where perfectionism is causing you stress. This journal will help you identify where these kinds of perfectionism show up in your life.

(This assessment is inspired by Hewitt and Flett's Multidimensional Perfectionism Scale.)

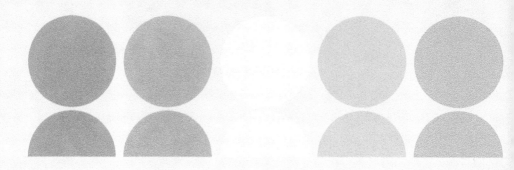

We can choose to be
perfect and admired or to
be real and loved.

—GLENNON DOYLE MELTON

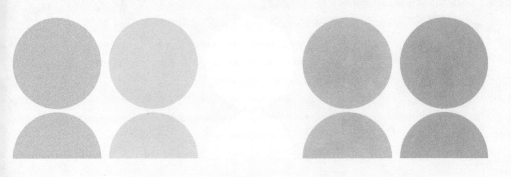

UNTANGLING PERFECTIONISM FROM WHO YOU ARE

Perfectionism can be like wearing a mask. Fear of being exposed as an impostor is how perfectionism can self-perpetuate. What would someone learn about you if you didn't need to be perfect?

_____

_____

_____

_____

_____

_____

What are some positive qualities you have that perfectionism doesn't allow you to showcase?

_____

_____

_____

_____

What would be the consequences for you of people seeing behind your perfection mask?

_____

_____

_____

_____

Perfectionism sometimes means you demand a lot from others, especially those closest to you. Having those demands might seem like you just have high standards, but it can be a way to keep others at arm's length so you don't get hurt. What are you afraid will happen if you relax your standards for others?

_____

_____

_____

_____

_____

_____

_____

_____

_____

_____

_____

_____

_____

_____

_____

_____

_____

_____

There can be a lot of pressure to maintain perfectionism, and some of the pressure comes from sources outside yourself. Do you come from a family or a culture that has certain expectations for you and your achievements? How do those expectations impact how you see yourself and your desire to be perfect? How would your relationships change if you weren't meeting those expectations?

Perfectionism develops over time, so it can be hard to imagine yourself without it. If you didn't believe you had to be perfect, what parts of your life would be different? What areas of your life would you pay more attention to? Give less attention to?

Do you believe you could be a successful person without being perfect? Why or why not?

_____

_____

_____

_____

_____

_____

_____

_____

_____

_____

_____

_____

_____

_____

_____

_____

_____

_____

_____

_____

What is perfectionism preventing you from doing or being? What are some things you'd want to pursue in your life if you weren't worried about doing them to perfection?

_____

_____

_____

_____

_____

_____

_____

_____

_____

_____

_____

_____

_____

_____

_____

_____

_____

_____

GAINING INSIGHT THROUGH MUSIC

Listening to music can help you gain new insights or put into words things or emotions you don't talk about. Music can allow perfectionists to experience and express emotions in a way that doesn't threaten the protective nature of perfectionism. For this activity, you will make yourself a playlist containing 15 songs.

1. Choose five songs that bring up happy and carefree memories from when you were growing up. These songs should transport you back to a moment when you were having fun: your first concert, a middle school dance, singing along with your family on a road trip, or dancing around your bedroom.

2. The next five songs should be your "pump-up" songs. When you hear these songs, you get motivated and inspired.

3. The last five songs should be your chill or calming songs. These are the songs you use to relax.

Listen to songs from your playlist. Reflect on any emotions that emerge and how they shift from song to song. Consider any themes that arise. Do the songs' lyrics have similar messages?

IDENTIFYING YOUR VALUES

One of the ways you make choices is **values-based decision-making**. Using the list provided on the next page, identify three values that are fed by your perfectionism. Consider both the positive and negative aspects of those values.

_____

_____

_____

Next, choose three values that you aspire to in your life. Think about how these aspirational values might conflict with your perfectionist values. Reflect on how you could integrate more of the former into your day-to-day life.

_____

_____

_____

Achievement	Friendship	Poise
Adventure	Fun	Popularity
Authenticity	Growth	Recognition
Authority	Happiness	Religion
Autonomy	Honesty	Reputation
Balance	Humor	Respect
Beauty	Influence	Responsibility
Boldness	Inner harmony	Security
Challenge	Justice	Self-respect
Citizenship	Kindness	Service
Community	Knowledge	Spirituality
Compassion	Leadership	Stability
Competency	Learning	Status
Contribution	Love	Success
Creativity	Loyalty	Trustworthiness
Curiosity	Meaningful work	Wealth
Determination	Openness	Wisdom
Fairness	Optimism	
Faith	Peace	
Fame	Pleasure	

Have no fear of perfection—
you'll never reach it.

—SALVADOR DALÍ

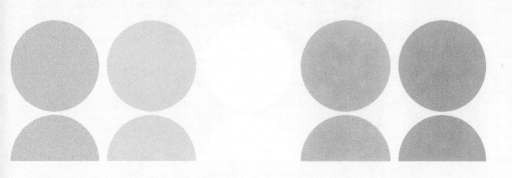

HOW SELF-ESTEEM AFFECTS PERFECTIONISM

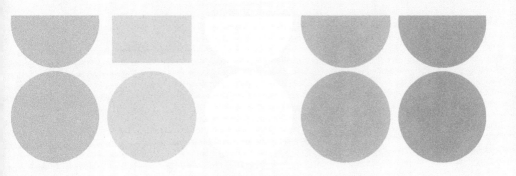

It can be hard to detangle your true nature from your perfectionism because perfectionism can feel like it provides the most efficient route to feeling good about yourself. How does perfectionism boost your self-esteem? Are there areas in your life that aren't "perfect" or that you feel ashamed of?

Perfectionists commonly rely on external validation for self-esteem. Accomplishments and accolades appear to improve self-esteem, but perfectionism requires you to chase them for fear of losing yourself without them. How have you been externally motivated? In school? At work? In relationships?

Comparing oneself with others is a common habit for perfectionists. This habit can make you view friends as "competition," as if there were some moral or material benefit to being more "perfect." Have you ever found yourself comparing your life with someone else's? If someone was more skilled or experienced than you in an area, were you jealous? How did you handle that feeling?

_____

_____

_____

_____

_____

_____

_____

_____

_____

_____

_____

_____

_____

_____

_____

_____

_____

Perfectionists are usually goal-oriented, and effective goal setting usually means that there's a time limit to achieve a goal. Do you have a timeline for your life? Have you accomplished your goals according to your timeline? If you haven't, how did it feel to miss a deadline? Has your expectation about when something should have been accomplished ever prevented you from enjoying an important event or milestone in your life?

What are some things you feel most proud of? What are some things you'd like to improve?

_____

_____

_____

_____

_____

_____

_____

_____

_____

_____

_____

_____

_____

_____

_____

_____

_____

_____

_____

_____

How does perfectionism impact your ability to be proud of yourself? What would happen to your self-esteem if you weren't perfect?

_____

_____

_____

_____

_____

_____

_____

_____

_____

_____

_____

_____

_____

_____

_____

_____

_____

_____

_____

_____

HAVING FUN WITH IMPERFECTION

Perfectionism robs you of the delight of being a novice and therefore can prevent you from trying new things that you might enjoy.

Try something new! Go to a new restaurant or coffee shop. Buy a trendy item that seems bold or daring. Sign up for music, art, or dance lessons. Give someone the benefit of the doubt when they don't meet your expectations.

Download an app to learn a new language or try meditation. The world is full of new things to try! Challenge perfectionism by being a novice and enjoy the process!

PROGRESS IS NEVER A STRAIGHT LINE

Perfectionism's desire for us to think in binary (black and white) and linear ways keeps us from being able to explore the nuances of our life's journey. Life is more like a corkscrew than a straight line. We move forward, backward, up, and down, but we do make progress.

- ☐ Take some time to think of five accomplishments.
- ☐ Plot those accomplishments on the straight line below, like a historical timeline.

L⎯⎯L⎯⎯L⎯⎯L⎯⎯L

- ☐ Plot your accomplishments on the corkscrew below.

- ☐ Think about where those accomplishments land on the corkscrew and what other things you had going on in your life. What propelled you? What held you back?

When you stop looking at your life as a straight line, you can begin to appreciate all aspects of yourself, not just the perfectionism that gets accolades and attention.

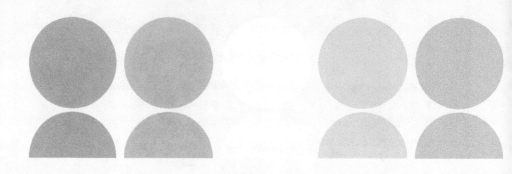

When you stop expecting
people to be perfect,
you can like them for who
they are.

—DONALD MILLER

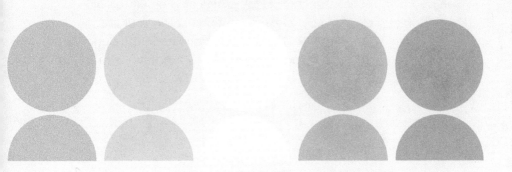

THE IMPACT OF
PERFECTIONISM ON
RELATIONSHIPS

Perfectionism is often about curating what you allow others to see about you—showing only certain parts of yourself to gain acceptance. Consider your closest relationships in your life: friends, family, romantic partners. What have been the benefits of allowing them to see you only as perfect? What have been the drawbacks?

Perfectionism is often reinforced because of the benefits you experience from striving for perfection. High achievement, notoriety, and popularity can all be by-products of perfectionism. In what ways do you think your friends impact your perfectionism? What about your family? Does your cultural background have any effect on your perfectionism?

_____

_____

_____

_____

_____

_____

_____

_____

_____

_____

_____

_____

_____

_____

_____

_____

_____

_____

Perfectionism sometimes shows up in relationships as unrealistic expectations for others, leading to conflict in relationships. Are you a grudge holder? What's preventing you from letting things go? How might your relationships change if you didn't hold grudges?

Perfectionism becomes isolating because it doesn't allow for deeper connections for fear of being "found out" as imperfect. How has perfectionism prevented you from growing closer to someone? Have you ever ended a relationship or friendship because you didn't want the other person to know too much about you for fear of their seeing you as imperfect?

Do you think your loved ones benefit from your perfectionism?
Why or why not?

_____

_____

_____

_____

_____

_____

_____

_____

_____

_____

_____

_____

_____

_____

_____

_____

_____

_____

_____

_____

Think about someone you care for deeply. If they made a mistake or were less than perfect, how would you react? What would you say or do because of their imperfection?

_____

_____

_____

_____

_____

_____

_____

_____

_____

_____

_____

_____

_____

_____

_____

_____

_____

_____

REDEFINING PERFECTION AND LOVE

Take some time to consider your definition of love. How would you describe the way you feel about the people, places, and things that you love?

Once you've defined love for yourself, think about your perfectionism. Define what perfectionism is for you. How does it show up in your life? How does it help or hinder?

Is your definition of love compatible with your definition of perfectionism? How might perfectionism be preventing you from enjoying the things you love because the definitions don't mesh?

JOHARI'S WINDOW

Johari's window is a visual representation to help you better understand your relationship with other people by highlighting the known and unknown parts of yourself. Johari's window has four boxes:

Known to Self + Known to Others (Known)

Known to Self + Unknown to Others (Hidden)

Unknown to Self + Known to Others (Blind Spot)

Unknown to Self + Unknown to Others (Unknown)

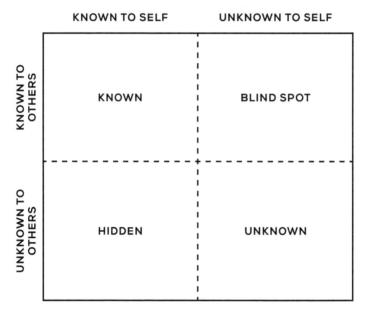

Take some time to think about yourself and fill out your Johari's window. When it comes to your unknown areas, think about the reflection you've done in this journal about your perfectionism.

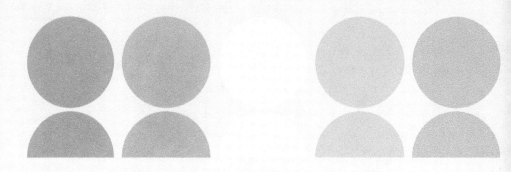

The pursuit of perfection
often impedes
improvement.

—GEORGE WILL

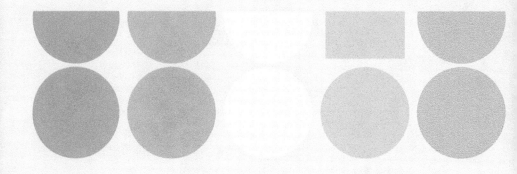

THE IMPACT OF PERFECTIONISM ON WORK, SCHOOL, OR VOCATION

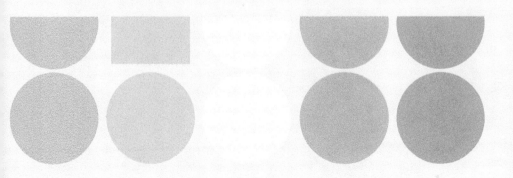

Perfectionism is self-perpetuating because initial positive gains reinforce the belief that we need to be perfect. Think about your accomplishments. Have any of the things you've achieved fed into your belief that you must be perfect?

_____

_____

_____

_____

_____

_____

_____

_____

_____

_____

_____

_____

_____

_____

_____

_____

_____

People whom you look up to can often unknowingly reinforce perfectionism. Think back to your childhood. Is there a memory that stands out to you where someone in your life made a negative comment or criticism about something you were proud of or when you tried your best? How did you feel receiving that negative feedback?

_____

_____

_____

_____

_____

_____

_____

_____

_____

_____

_____

_____

_____

_____

Perfectionists often become leaders in different parts of their lives because of their desire to achieve and their track record of excellence. Have you ever been in a leadership role? Did you expect the people you were leading to do tasks or activities the way you would do them, or did you let them have their own methods? How did you respond if folks you were leading disagreed with you?

_____

_____

_____

_____

_____

_____

_____

_____

_____

_____

_____

_____

_____

_____

_____

_____

The desire to be perfect can lead to things like good grades, promotions, awards, etc. But sustaining perfection as a standard will eventually lead to burnout. Have you ever felt burned out? How did you handle it? Did your job, school, or reputation suffer as you healed from burnout?

_____

_____

_____

_____

_____

_____

_____

_____

_____

_____

_____

_____

_____

_____

_____

_____

_____

_____

_____

_____

_____

Has there ever been a time when your desire to be perfect caused you to miss out on something fun or important at work or school, or with your family or friends?

_____

_____

_____

_____

_____

_____

_____

_____

_____

_____

_____

_____

_____

_____

_____

_____

_____

_____

Perfectionists often want to give 100 percent to their work. What would the consequences be if you gave only 90 percent? Or 60 percent? What percentage could you land at in your life and still achieve your goals?

BUSTING BUSY WITH
A BOUNDARY

Perfectionists often build their identities around what they do and what they accomplish. This makes setting boundaries tough but important.

Pick something related to work or school to set a boundary around. Ideas may include: no checking email after seven p.m.; submitting a project or assignment that's "good enough"; no working on weekends.

This exercise is not about the boundary itself. Setting the boundary and maintaining it will bring up thoughts and feelings about your self-worth, productivity, and perfectionism that you may have been avoiding by staying "busy." What comes up for you? Do any reactions surprise you? Journal about whatever comes up as you maintain that boundary.

LETTER TO YOUR YOUNGER SELF

Think about your younger self. Pick a specific instance when you felt like what you were offering wasn't good enough for an adult in your life. What is that moment? What happened? How did you feel?

Now, with all your experience, expertise, and knowledge of how the world really works, write a letter to that child. Write the things you needed to hear when you were in that situation. We gain resilience as children when there is more than one voice to listen to, so give your childhood self an opportunity to have that voice of care and encouragement that you deserved.

This may be an emotional experience for you. Allow yourself the time and space to experience the emotions that come up for you as you complete this exercise. Remember, you are both the writer and the receiver of this letter, so all emotions are valid as you complete this activity.

Perfectionism rarely begets
perfection, or satisfaction—
only disappointment.

—RYAN HOLIDAY

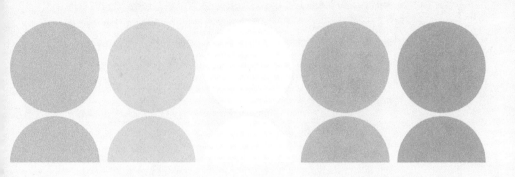

THE IMPACT OF PERFECTIONISM ON YOUR HEALTH AND WELLNESS

Toxic stress is when stress slowly but continually builds up and your brain and body learn to expect stress to be there, so it feels odd, or even wrong, to be relaxed. Perfectionism feeds the cycle when anything less than perfection is disappointing. Have you ever felt disappointed or angry about not being the best, even though you objectively did well?

Perfectionism can prevent you from reaching out for help for fear of being perceived as imperfect. Have you ever gone to a doctor's office or a therapy appointment and not told the whole story out of fear that your provider might judge you? What consequences were you afraid of that prevented you from being more transparent?

Perfectionism sometimes means we judge others for being less than perfect. Have you ever made negative assumptions about someone because you didn't think they were living a healthy life? What about their behaviors, bodies, or conditions prompted you to pass judgment?

_____

_____

_____

_____

_____

_____

_____

_____

_____

_____

_____

_____

_____

_____

_____

_____

_____

_____

Striving for perfection sometimes means ignoring the signs that something's wrong. Have you ever put off seeking treatment for a medical or mental health symptom because you didn't want to believe that there was anything wrong? Were there any consequences for making that choice?

Have you ever pushed through physical pain in exercise or sporting events to win or finish? Why was finishing or winning more important than taking care of yourself?

_____

_____

_____

_____

_____

_____

_____

_____

_____

_____

_____

_____

_____

_____

_____

_____

_____

_____

_____

_____

Do you think that striving for perfection helps or hinders your ability to be happy in your life? Why?

_____

_____

_____

_____

_____

_____

_____

_____

_____

_____

_____

_____

_____

_____

_____

_____

_____

_____

_____

_____

PROGRESSIVE MUSCLE RELAXATION

Sometimes we don't realize we're holding on to stress and tension in our bodies until we can experience relief. Progressive muscle relaxation can help you experience the contrast between tight and relaxed muscles so you can ease tension in your body, soothe anxiety, and refocus.

1. Start by lying down or sitting in a chair.

2. Begin with your feet: Curl your toes and tighten the arches of your feet. Hold for 5 to 10 seconds, and release.

3. Tighten your calves for 5 to 10 seconds. Release.

4. Tighten your thighs and buttocks for 5 to 10 seconds. Release.

5. Tighten your abs in the front, then the muscles in your lower back. Hold for 5 to 10 seconds. Release.

6. Tighten your chest and upper back for 5 to 10 seconds. Release.

7. Tense your arms by squeezing your hands into fists and tightening your biceps. Hold for 5 to 10 seconds. Release.

8. Scrunch up your face and hold for 5 to 10 seconds. Release.

9. Last, tense your entire body all at once. Hold for as long as you comfortably can, then release.

SOCIAL MEDIA AUDIT

Every day there's more information coming out about how social media deeply influences how we think and feel about ourselves. You might be drawn to accounts that have beautifully curated content made by people who show only the perfect parts of themselves, with the occasional "I'm not so perfect, and here's my pile of laundry to prove it" posts. It may all seem like harmless scrolling, but you might be reinforcing a negative self-image and perfectionism.

- ☐ Take some time to audit who you follow on social media.

- ☐ Unfollow any account that's prompted jealousy or negative feelings about yourself. If you miss their content in a week, you can always refollow them.

- ☐ Go follow something that aligns with the values you explored on page 21. Maybe it's a social cause or local nonprofit. Maybe it's an account of someone who doesn't look, think, or act like you and you're interested in learning more about their perspective.

- ☐ Diversify your scroll.

Periodically doing this with your social media accounts will help prevent the reinforcement of perfectionism and open you up to new ideas and experiences.

Before I built a wall
I'd ask to know
What I was walling in
or walling out,
And to whom I was like
to give offense.

—ROBERT FROST

WHAT IS PERFECTIONISM PROTECTING YOU FROM?

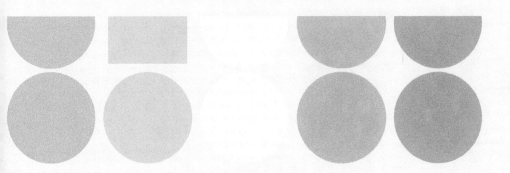

Perfectionism develops as a response to unpleasant experiences or emotions. What experiences or emotions do you avoid by being perfect? Why do you believe those experiences or emotions should be avoided?

_____

_____

_____

_____

_____

_____

_____

_____

_____

_____

_____

_____

_____

_____

_____

_____

_____

_____

Popularity can be seen as essential for survival because we are social beings that need a sense of belonging to feel safe. Have you ever tried to hide parts of yourself from others in order to fit in and gain acceptance? Would you make the same choices if you had to do it over?

_____

_____

_____

_____

_____

_____

_____

_____

_____

_____

_____

_____

_____

_____

_____

_____

_____

_____

_____

Social hierarchies are designed to create in-groups and out-groups. Have you ever gone out of your way to point out something in someone else that put them in the "out" category? Did you feel like it was necessary to leave someone out so you would be "in"?

_____

_____

_____

_____

_____

_____

_____

_____

_____

_____

_____

_____

_____

_____

_____

_____

Perfectionism can develop as a coping strategy to protect oneself from rejection or have control by earning acceptance through accomplishments. How has striving for perfection gained you acceptance? In what ways do you think being perfect protects you from rejection or gives you control?

Some perfectionists believe that if they keep achieving something new, they will always be "one step ahead." What do you think you are trying to stay ahead of? How does staying ahead make your life better?

_____

_____

_____

_____

_____

_____

_____

_____

_____

_____

_____

_____

_____

_____

_____

_____

Perfectionists often view themselves negatively and are overly critical of themselves. Have you ever been very critical of yourself in a situation where you wouldn't have been critical of someone else in a similar situation? Why?

_____

_____

_____

_____

_____

_____

_____

_____

_____

_____

_____

_____

_____

_____

_____

_____

_____

SEEKING SAFETY

This practice will help you create a place of safety in your mind that you can revisit anytime.

1. Think of a place you've always wanted to go. It could be a place you've wanted to travel to or a place from fiction that seems wonderful.

2. Close your eyes and allow yourself to experience that place.

3. What do you see? Smell? Hear? Feel? What is the weather like? Indulge every sense and try to absorb this place. See if you can make the details more vivid as you experience them in your mind.

4. Now concentrate on your emotions. Allow yourself to connect with feelings of calmness, peace, safety, and security. Where do you feel the emotions in your body?

5. Give a name to this place. This place will always be available to you, and those peaceful feelings will grow stronger as you practice the exercise.

Having a place of safety in your brain can help when you feel overwhelmed or bogged down by perfectionism.

FROM HEAD CRITIC TO CHEER CAPTAIN

Perfectionism usually means that there's a constant critic living in your head, doling out criticism and snarky comments. In internal family systems therapy there is a belief that we all have "parts" of ourselves, and that our critical "parts" are actually cheerleaders that have been forced into the role of critic. Let's turn your critic back into a cheerleader.

- ☐ Think back to a time when something wasn't perfect or didn't go according to plan.

- ☐ Using the table provided on the next page, write down five critical thoughts about yourself and that situation.

- ☐ Now write down five things you could say to yourself if you were your biggest cheerleader instead of your biggest critic.

Challenge yourself to be genuinely kind and empathetic to yourself about that event. If you're having trouble being kind, think about what you might say to a friend who just said something self-critical about a similar issue. It sometimes helps you to depersonalize it, get some distance from your own experience, and then apply that to yourself.

THE EVENT:		
	CRITIC	**CHEERLEADER**
THOUGHT 1		
THOUGHT 2		
THOUGHT 3		
THOUGHT 4		
THOUGHT 5		

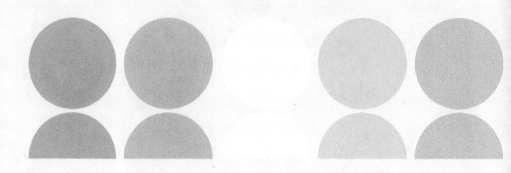

People throw away what they could have by insisting on perfection, which they cannot have, and looking for it where they will never find it.

—EDITH SCHAEFFER

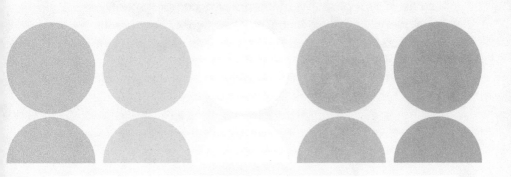

USING THE
BENEFITS AND
AVOIDING THE
PITFALLS OF
PERFECTIONISM

Perfectionism often goes hand in hand with achievement. What are some of your proudest moments or accomplishments? In your relationships? Your schooling? Your work? Your health and wellness? How did your high standards contribute to these achievements?

Perfectionism can give you a positive reputation, because perfectionists usually work hard and get positive results. What are some of the positive ways people might describe you if they were asked about you? How has your reputation for excellence helped you in various aspects of your life?

A perfectionist's desire for perfection usually doesn't stop at themselves; they want to surround themselves with others who strive for perfection. Think of the five people in your life whom you're closest to. What do you admire about them? How do they encourage you?

_____

_____

_____

_____

_____

_____

_____

_____

_____

_____

_____

_____

_____

_____

_____

_____

_____

_____

Perfectionism can cause people to turn inward and become self-conscious, self-absorbed, and sometimes selfish. Think about a time when your desire to be perfect prevented you from noticing the needs or desires of others. How might you handle the situation differently in the future or make amends for it now?

_____

_____

_____

_____

_____

_____

_____

_____

_____

_____

_____

_____

_____

_____

_____

_____

_____

_____

Think of three areas in your life where exchanging perfect standards for good enough would immediately make you feel less stressed.

_____

_____

_____

How can you begin to incorporate the insight you're gaining from this book to help you live a more balanced life? What needs to change? What would you like to keep?

_____

_____

_____

_____

_____

_____

_____

_____

_____

_____

_____

_____

_____

_____

JOYFUL MOVEMENT

Stress from perfectionism can get stuck in your body, and chronic stress wreaks havoc on your mental, emotional, and physical wellness.

One of the most effective ways to process the physical impacts of stress on your body is movement.

1. Turn on the music you love and move your body. No one expects it to be pretty. You're not auditioning for *Swan Lake*, you just need to move the stress chemicals through.

2. You can do this sitting down or even in your car.

3. It can be as simple as tapping your toes and bobbing your head to the beat.

4. Just get your body going to a song that makes you want to move!

You'll feel better by the time the song ends.

FINDING YOUR FOUNDATION

As you gain more insight into the issues that perfectionism has caused, it can be startling to realize that a lot of the things you thought you knew about yourself may no longer fit, or you want them to change. This activity is designed to help you move forward with a deeper, more meaningful sense of yourself.

- ☐ Pick five traits, qualities, or quirks about yourself that you're proud of. You can look back at the previous values exercise on page 21 if you want to incorporate your values into your sense of self.

- ☐ For each quality or trait, think about a time when you've demonstrated that quality.

Example:

I am brave. I know that is true because I moved somewhere new and established an amazing life with awesome people in my new city.

Your turn:

I am ——————— . I know this is true because ———————— .

I am ——————— . I know this is true because ———————— .

I am ——————— . I know this is true because ———————— .

I am ——————— . I know this is true because ———————— .

I am ——————— . I know this is true because ———————— .

The most beautiful things are
not perfect, they are special.

—BOB MARLEY

HOW
PERFECTIONISM
DISCONNECTS US

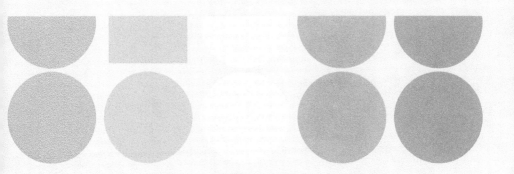

Perfectionists often separate themselves from others by being exceptional, but that separateness can also create loneliness. Reflect on your achievements; did they make you feel more or less connected to others? Why?

_____

_____

_____

_____

_____

_____

_____

_____

_____

_____

_____

_____

_____

_____

_____

Perfection is sometimes the standard that we believe others have for us. Think about the people who reinforce your perfectionism, both overtly and covertly. Do these expectations from others ever inhibit your relationship with them? Have you ever felt resentful or frustrated about others' expectations of you? Why or why not?

_____

_____

_____

_____

_____

_____

_____

_____

_____

_____

_____

_____

_____

_____

Perfectionism in relationships often manifests as loving someone's potential instead of loving where they are right now. Have you ever seen someone's potential and been frustrated because they didn't seem interested in fulfilling it? How did your desire for them to achieve impact the relationship?

_____

_____

_____

_____

_____

_____

_____

_____

_____

_____

_____

_____

_____

_____

_____

_____

_____

Perfectionism inhibits your relationship with yourself and your intuition, because perfectionism redirects attention to focus only on activities and people that reinforce perfectionism. Being narrowly focused on achievement requires you to block out the many connections you have between your body, mind, and emotions. When is the last time you had a "gut" instinct? Did you follow it? Why or why not? Did your instinct reinforce or challenge your perfectionism?

What are some areas in your life you would like to be more connected?

_____

_____

_____

_____

_____

_____

_____

_____

_____

_____

_____

_____

_____

_____

_____

_____

_____

_____

_____

What are some ways you can practice being more connected to your desired areas in your life on a monthly, a weekly, and a daily basis?

_____

_____

_____

_____

_____

_____

_____

_____

_____

_____

_____

_____

_____

_____

_____

_____

MEASURED BREATHING

Perfectionism can rob you of connection by limiting your presence in the moment. One of the most effective ways to reconnect to the present is through breathing. This breathing exercise requires you to focus on your breathing and has the added benefit of slowing down your heart rate and relaxing your nervous system.

1. Begin by taking three deep breaths at your own pace.

2. On the fourth breath, breathe in as you silently count one, two, three, four, five.

3. Hold the breath while you silently count one, two, three, four, five, six.

4. Breathe out slowly while you silently count one, two, three, four, five, six, seven.

5. Repeat three times, or until you are feeling calmer and more focused in the present moment.

FEEL CONNECTED

Feeling connected is important for your emotional and social well-being, but it's also necessary for your survival. Part of how perfectionism distorts your understanding of connection is that it gets you thinking that you have to stand out in order to be part of the group. But sometimes it's nice to be one of many.

Make a list of 10 activities that you prefer to do with others and that have nothing to do with being perfect.

Examples:

Concerts   *Dinner with friends*   *Bowling*

_____

_____

_____

_____

_____

_____

_____

_____

_____

_____

From the moment perfection
is attained, 'tis gone.

—IVAN PANIN

WHEN PERFECTIONISM DISTORTS YOUR EXPECTATIONS

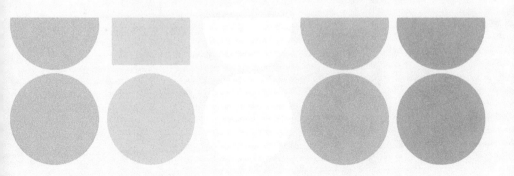

Challenging perfectionistic beliefs can help reduce the negative impact of perfectionism. When you challenge perfectionistic beliefs, you're standing up for yourself and your abilities, which improves trust and connection to yourself and others. To challenge perfectionistic beliefs, you must first identify them. What are some of the beliefs you have about being perfect that have begun to emerge as you've participated in this journal?

In the previous section (see page 89), you thought about how other people's expectations of you have impacted your relationships with them. Have you ever told them how you feel about their expectations of you? What would it be like to share how their expectations impact you and your relationship with them?

Think about someone you're close to that you have high expectations for. How would you respond if they shared that your expectations are inhibiting your relationship with them? What might you change about how you communicate with them? Would your expectations change?

Perfectionism can develop as a defense mechanism to protect yourself from other people's judgments, but you ultimately have no control over them. Would you feel the need to be perfect if you let go of what other people think about you? How might you begin to release yourself from your own perception of other people's opinions?

_____

_____

_____

_____

_____

_____

_____

_____

_____

_____

_____

_____

_____

_____

_____

_____

_____

_____

What is the impact of perfectionism on your stress level? What do you think would happen to your stress level if you didn't feel pressure to be perfect?

_____

_____

_____

_____

_____

_____

_____

_____

_____

_____

_____

_____

_____

_____

_____

_____

_____

_____

What are some ways you've learned to handle stress effectively? What are some things you've wanted to try to help you feel less stressed but haven't? What's held you back?

_____

_____

_____

_____

_____

_____

_____

_____

_____

_____

_____

_____

_____

_____

_____

_____

STANDING IN YOUR TRUTH

Take some moments to stand in a quiet place, without shoes.

1. Begin by standing with your feet about hip-width apart and your hands at your sides.

2. Turn both of your palms facing forward and extend your arms slightly to each side.

3. You are now in Mountain Pose—a grounding, foundational pose in yoga.

4. Breathe deeply, in and out, for a few breaths.

5. Say a positive affirmation to yourself. It can be in your head or out loud.

   Examples could include:

   - *I am worthy of love and rest.*

   - *I am fine the way I am.*

   - *I am content with my life.*

6. Repeat your affirmations a few times and indulge in the strength and power of being grounded in your body and your mind with positivity.

BALANCING PERFECTIONIST BELIEFS

Changing your beliefs can be a slow process. The fastest way to achieve long-term-belief shifts is to try to find a *balanced* belief. It's sometimes harder to find a balanced belief than an extreme one. This activity will help you identify balanced beliefs by finding the perfectionist belief and the opposite belief first, then moving toward the balanced belief.

PERFECTIONIST BELIEF	OPPOSITE BELIEF	BALANCED BELIEF
I need to look perfect to leave the house.	I don't care how I look when I leave the house.	Looking presentable is important to me, but I don't have to be perfect.
I can't leave work until this project meets my high standards.	The quality of my work doesn't matter.	If I focus on completing a project, I can go back and make edits.

Possessing the ideal makes
a person nervous: you
sense the inevitable decline
just ahead.

—GARRISON KEILLOR

THE LIMITED VALUE
OF POTENTIAL

Think about an object in your life that you love. It could be your favorite childhood stuffed animal or a pair of perfectly broken-in shoes. Describe what it is and why you love it.

_____

_____

_____

Is the object perfect? Would anyone else think this thing is perfect? Why or why not?

_____

_____

_____

_____

_____

_____

_____

_____

_____

_____

_____

_____

Often the seeds of perfectionism develop in childhood to help make sense of the expectations of others. Think back to when you were a child. Did you excel at something? Did your ability to excel in that area limit you from growing in other areas because of your narrow focus? Or did you have a general need to be perfect at everything, so you avoided new things? How has perfectionism limited your potential?

When a team leader is a perfectionist, it can be very damaging because the creativity, perspectives, and values that others on the team bring to the table are overwhelmed by the perfectionist expectations of the leader. Have you ever been on a team where you were stifled by someone else's high expectations? Have you ever been the one with the expectations and learned the hard way through team conflict or issues with delivering a final product?

Self-doubt goes hand in hand with perfectionism. Have you ever been stuck between thinking you could have done so much more or better and feeling paralyzed by the belief that you weren't good enough to begin with? How did you handle having those two opposing thoughts trying to take up the same space?

_____

_____

_____

_____

_____

_____

_____

_____

_____

_____

_____

_____

_____

_____

_____

_____

_____

_____

Overvaluing potential is like living off of credit cards; the bill will come due. How can you balance the "budget" of potential and actual ability in your life?

_____

_____

_____

_____

_____

_____

_____

_____

_____

_____

_____

_____

_____

_____

_____

_____

_____

_____

Do you give yourself enough credit for having improved over time? What are some ways you've grown over the past six months? Year? Five years?

CALLING OUT YOUR PERFECTIONISM

Perfectionists often believe that others are perfect and that the bar for everyone is incredibly high, and they tend to ignore evidence that suggests that being perfect isn't the expectation. Think about your mentor or someone you look up to who has given you wise counsel. Call, email, or write to this person and ask them about a time they made a mistake and how they recovered from it. I think you'll be surprised at the mistakes and missteps that folks have overcome to be where they are today. Also ask them if they believe that the mistake they shared with you contained a valuable lesson. It's likely that they not only made that mistake, but it also allowed them to grow in ways that they couldn't have without the mistake.

BECOMING MULTIFACETED

When working to unlearn perfectionism, it becomes vital to allow many things to be true for you at the same time. It can be true that you tried your best at the same time that you didn't win first place. It can be true that you could have spent more time perfecting something at work and that you had social obligations to attend. It can be true that your coach wanted you to have fun while playing a sport and that they wanted you to get better at the sport. When you can identify multiple things as true at the same time, the perfectionist thoughts and beliefs lose their strength, because those are just some of many things that can be true.

Use the gems below to explore the many facets of your life. Write down truths for each gem, and begin to expose the flaws in perfectionist thinking. Just like gemstones, we need facets to help us reveal our sparkle and shine.

RELATIONSHIPS

WORK

HEALTH & WELLNESS

I am careful not to confuse
excellence with perfection.

—MICHAEL J. FOX

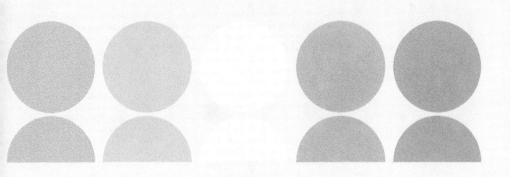

UNDOING THE LONG-TERM IMPACT OF PERFECTIONISM

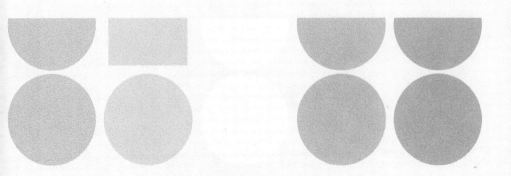

Perfectionism creates a false sense of security while chipping away at your true sense of self. Think about a time in your life when you had joy that wasn't attached to an achievement. What was that moment? What felt special to you about that moment? How can you have more moments like that one?

The guilt of disappointing others can perpetuate perfectionism. When is the last time you felt guilty because you thought you'd let someone down? Was the expectation placed on you reasonable or unreasonable? Were you an active participant in setting that expectation? Are you taking on responsibility for the other person's emotions about your behavior?

Wanting others to be perfect allows you to be justified in your disappointment if others don't meet your standards. Have you ever held resentment toward someone because they chose not to meet your expectations? How did you feel about that situation? Now that you've explored your perfectionism in this journal, how would you choose to handle a similar situation in the future?

Perfectionism slowly shifts your thoughts to believing that things aren't worth doing or pursuing if perfection or mastery doesn't come quickly. Is there anything you've wanted to try but you've been afraid of "not doing it right"? Does perfectionism prevent you from doing things that you know might benefit you (like meditation, yoga, trying to cook new foods, traveling, or joining a dating app)?

_____

_____

_____

_____

_____

_____

_____

_____

_____

_____

_____

_____

_____

_____

_____

_____

_____

For many people, perfectionism impacts their thoughts and beliefs about how they look. Do you have a positive, negative, or neutral relationship with your body? How did the relationship become that way?

What are some ways you can work to improve your relationship with your body and body image?

_____

_____

_____

_____

_____

_____

_____

_____

_____

_____

_____

_____

_____

_____

_____

_____

_____

_____

_____

LOVE YOUR "FLAWS"

Think about the parts of your body that you feel self-conscious about. As a perfectionist, you've probably spent more time thinking about how to change those parts of yourself and not very much time working to embrace them.

Over the next 24 hours, take some time to thank your body, especially the parts that you're self-conscious about. For example, if you think your thighs are too big, thank your legs for helping you walk and get around.

CREATING AN IMPERFECT VISION

Create a vision board of what you could do without perfectionism. You can use poster board and magazines, create a Pinterest board, or make a bookmark folder in your browser.

- What would you wear if you weren't afraid of having your style judged?

- What haircut would you get?

- Where would you travel to if you weren't letting perfectionism hold you back?

- What hobbies would you try?

- Where would you live?

- Who would you be friends with?

Think about all the things you want in your life that your idea of perfect is holding you back from. Dream really big. Your fantastic, imperfect life is waiting for you!

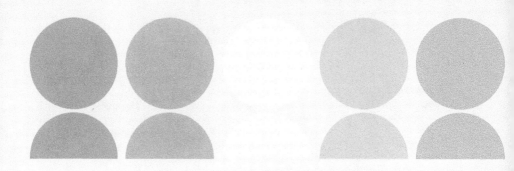

One of the basic rules of
the universe is that nothing
is perfect. Perfection simply
doesn't exist . . . Without
imperfection, neither you nor
I would exist.

—STEPHEN HAWKING

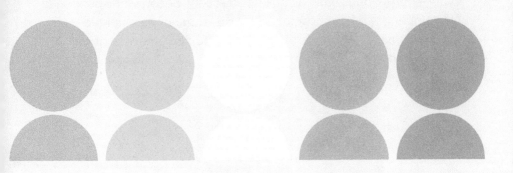

EMBRACING IMPERFECTIONS AND LOVING YOURSELF

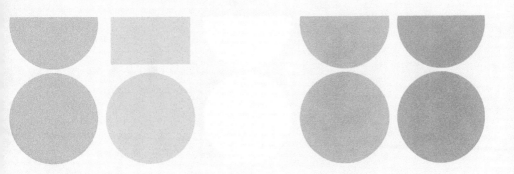

There is a concept in Japanese culture called *wabi-sabi*.
Wabi-sabi is about embracing imperfections because they allow
for uniqueness and character. What are some of your unique
qualities? What are some of the things you can embrace about
yourself that make you unique and special, even if they're not
perfect?

_____

_____

_____

_____

_____

_____

_____

_____

_____

_____

_____

_____

_____

_____

_____

_____

Perfectionists are often their own worst critics. Recall the thoughts you wrote down in the critic-to-cheerleader activity (see page 73). Now imagine saying some of those thoughts to your best friend, your parents, your mentor, or someone you work with. Would you have said anything like that to any of those people? Why or why not?

_____

_____

_____

_____

_____

_____

_____

_____

_____

_____

_____

_____

_____

_____

_____

_____

_____

_____

As a perfectionist, you may want the people you love to be successful, and you might sometimes give advice or impose your beliefs onto others without asking if it's wanted. Have you ever given unsolicited advice to someone you care about? How did the person respond? Did they take the advice? What are some other ways that you could show support or concern without giving advice?

Perfectionism is a time thief. The amount of time it takes to "achieve perfection" adds up, whether it's perfecting a project, your look for the day, or what you're going to say in a conversation later to impress people. It takes away time you could spend on something else. How would you prefer to spend those extra moments that perfectionism steals from you?

Have you ever been too tired to be perfect? Has trying to perfect something left you feeling exhausted after your task was completed? How did it feel to have that experience?

_____

_____

_____

_____

_____

_____

_____

_____

_____

_____

_____

_____

_____

_____

_____

_____

What are some things you could drop from your schedule if you weren't striving for perfection?

_____

_____

_____

_____

_____

_____

_____

_____

_____

_____

_____

_____

_____

_____

_____

_____

_____

_____

_____

_____

GATHERING GRATITUDE

Write a list of seven things you're grateful for. Every day for one week, pick one of those things and spend 10 minutes experiencing your gratitude for that thing. Your experience could be in meditation, journaling, or looking at photos if it's a person, place, or pet.

EVERY PANCAKE
HAS TWO SIDES

Just like every pancake has two sides, every asset has a flaw, and every flaw can be an asset.

Think about the flaws you think you have. Write down a list of flaws, and then put your brain to work on how they might be assets. The asset doesn't have to be constant, but how might that flaw help you from time to time?

FLAW	ASSET
Worry	*I make sure things around me are safe.*

CLOSING NOTE

Untangling perfectionism from your life can be a long and complex journey, but you have taken amazing strides forward by completing this journal.

There are many ways to work on relieving the stress of perfectionism, and I hope that the momentum you gained from this journal will move you into the next chapter of your life and a new relationship with perfectionism.

If you found this journal challenging or painful to complete, I recommend speaking to a counselor or therapist about what came up for you. Even if you weren't able to complete all the prompts or activities, you did gain valuable insight into tender parts of yourself that having some therapeutic support could be helpful in healing.

This journal was directly inspired by the work I've done with my own clients to help with their healing from perfectionism, but it's okay if not every prompt, activity, or practice spoke directly to you and your perfectionism. As my clients in Alcoholics Anonymous and Narcotics Anonymous say, "If it doesn't apply, let it fly." That being said, I hope that you will circle back to some of the questions or activities that didn't pertain to you initially. As you continue on your healing journey, you may find that some of the things that didn't apply this time resonate with you later on. You are, and shall remain, a beautifully imperfect work in progress.

RESOURCES

Books

Emotional Agility, Susan David, PhD: Breaks down the experi-ence of getting emotionally "hooked" and provides practical ways to become more emotionally agile.

Nervous Energy, Dr. Chloe Carmichael, PhD: Dr. Chloe explains brain/body connections and how to use anxiety and the energy it produces to your benefit.

Pedagogy of the Oppressed, Paulo Freire: This book explores self-liberation, community building, and new ways to think about education and learning.

Apps

Insight Timer: This app allows you to access an enormous library of mindfulness meditations, lessons, and exercises from contrib-utors around the world who are working on mindfulness.

Podcasts

Home Cooking, Samin Nosrat and Hrishikesh Hirway: This podcast is about cooking, but perfectionists can learn a lot from listening to the hosts discuss the mistakes they made in their cooking over the years and how they bounced back from disappointment.

Maintenance Phase, Aubrey Gordon and Michael Hobbes: This podcast debunks health and wellness trends with charming hosts and tons of well-researched topics, such as bodies, self-image, and wellness.

REFERENCES

Esposito, R. P., H. Mcadoo, and L. Scher. "The Johari Window Test: A Research Note." *Journal of Humanistic Psychology* 18, no. 1 (1978): 79–81. doi:10.1177/002216787801800113.

Hewitt, P. L., and G. L. Flett. "Perfectionism and Depression: A Multidimensional Analysis." *Journal of Social Behavior and Personality* 5 (1990), 423–38.

Shapiro, F. *Eye Movement Desensitization and Reprocessing (EMDR) Therapy: Basic Principles, Protocols, and Procedures* (Guilford Press, 2018).

ACKNOWLEDGMENTS

To John for being an amazing partner, my best friend, and greatest supporter.

To my Kocol aunts, who always demonstrate kindness, creativity, perseverance, and humor.

To Chuck for telling me my dreams were too small in the rudest way possible.

To my friends, who teach me about embracing imperfection and accepting unconditional love.

To my clients, who consistently inspire me with their resilience and commitment to healing.

And to Ben, who desperately needed this book. I miss you all the time.

ABOUT THE AUTHOR

TINA KOCOL, LPC, is a trauma therapist specializing in EMDR and group therapies in Philadelphia. In her private practice, Green Circle Collective, she works with a wide variety of perfectionists in therapy and workshops. She has a passion for helping people become who they always dreamed of being before perfectionism set in. Her dream is to develop a cooperative practice of multidisciplinary trauma healers and to provide recovery for anyone who needs it—all in a glorious greenhouse and a farm retreat center. When she's not working, Tina loves to garden, cook for people she loves, and search for great iced coffee.

CPSIA information can be obtained
at www.ICGtesting.com
Printed in the USA
BVHW061114280322
632107BV00002B/6